There's Nowt Th

By Floyd Coggins

Copyright F Coggins 2018.

All Rights Reserved.

Dawson mc.

We're on our way to see my Grandad
He lives up north in a town that is way out of the way.
The idea, so dad tells me, is to persuade him to come
Down to our house to stay.

But Grandads not one to travel and I know he's not
Going to be pleased
Whenever I mention our town he says Milton Keynes
"There's nowt there but trees."

I've tried to tell him that it has changed
Since the last time he came down to stay
And if he just came down for the weekend
It might help to change his way.

But he just sits in that stupid old armchair
And I swear he just says it to tease.
"I'm not coming down and that's final
I've told you there's nowt down there but trees."

And then he goes on
"Yer Dad tells me he's got some fancy job
But I know he's just out to deceive
It must take whole population all flaming year
to pick up autumn leaves.

So if yer don't mind, I'll stay here where I can see horizon
Yer welcome to stay here if you please,
But don't tell me about some fancy new city
Cos I know there's nowt there but trees."

<u>JESUS</u>

BORN

CHERISHED

ADORED

WOSHIPPED

FOLLOWED

FEARED

BETRAYED

FALLEN

RISEN

The magic ingredient

There is a magic ingredient missing
When I look at another girl
A mild glance of interest I grant you
As I peer at her unknowing twirl,
But no more than a hint of curiosity
Would my heart say could ever be due.
For the magic ingredient that is missing
Is that something special I know only as you.

They came in their thousands

They came in their thousands
They came in droves
Across fields through valleys
Along rivers and roads.
In search of a vision
An unfulfilled dream
A new way of living
Or just a new scene.

As grass turned to mud
And mud turned to stone
A city arose from the
Toils of its own.
Now a new generation
Both native and bred
Stands well prepared
For the future ahead.

For they alone will know
What it will all mean
To have lived, loved and died
In Milton Keynes.

The garden fence

The politics of division
a barrier to peace.
An urban border between two nations
to defend and police.
An idealistic vision of what is ours,
that leads us to behave
like savages under threat from a lone invading brave.
Regarded with suspicion the neighbour stakes his claim,
Eager eyes upon him should he attempt to gain.
A downtrodden bush, a stolen inch,
a fallen tool upon a flower,
sets off a rage in an upstairs room
that serves as a watchtower.
The wooden wall of anger now stands there good and true.
The rulers of all our kingdom and all that we can view.
But if we cannot befriend our neighbours,
If we cannot fill this niche,
what hope have we of achieving the dream that is
world peace.

FLICKERING SHADOW

Flickering shadow dancing across the hall,
into the bedroom and under the bed,
then out through the wall.

Folding, stretching, shrinking, turning-
there seems to be no limit to your form,
up onto the ceiling then down onto the floor,
quite suddenly you disappear, I turn, and you are reborn.

Yet who is this other person?
This other me, that dares to imitate my every move
with a mere parody?

But this darkened patch of anti-light
shows a remarkable resistance
that brings a comfort to my soul,
for it serves as confirmation of my own existence.

ARCADES AND ALLEYWAYS

The arcades and alleyways that cross my troubled mind
and reek of my existence.
Serve to hide my evil past, where shattered souls who
put their trust in me lie lost and undefended, amongst
the heaps of rotting memories that I have disregarded.
No respect for life nor love I lived only for my
Self- advancement.
But now my once able body has turned against me,
my life is now under threat.
Called to account for what I cannot answer and will not justify.
What god would invite me into his heaven when my soul
is blacker than an endless night.
What hell would recommend me to its master when I am
More deserving of his crown.
Am I to live the second life suspended between two worlds
with no claim upon my soul.
or could I find forgiveness for the unforgivable in a love
I have yet to know.

THE VASE WITHIN MY ROOM

No daffodil or hyacinth
Could ever find a place
In the garden of my fantasy
That I would fill to suit
Only my taste.

No roses there to grow and bloom
No tulips to fill me with delight
For these gems of mother earth
Would somehow, not seem right.

No trees of majesty with leaves that hold on fast
Yet come September's breeze would fall to stain
The autumn grass.
No ferns with foliage soft and green that is a
Wonder to us all.
No daisies or buttercups and no sweet peas to climb
The garden wall.

For among the borders and the beds
Only one flower would be found
For there would grow the seeds of you
That I had sown there in the ground.
And often I would walk among the fragrant buds
And bloom to gather up your beauty to fill the vase
Within my room.

And it is there that I would tend to you
Until your fragile stem should wither
Then out into my garden again I would go
Your beauty there to gather.

LATE AT NIGHT

Late at night I lie awake
and I turn to your sweet face
I wonder?

If you were gone where would I be
and what would this life hold in store for
for me ?

As I travel on and on through life's fantasy
I ponder for a while as the truth is plain to see.
Loneliness, unhappiness, misery and despair,
a world of lost beginnings
Devoid of any care.

Late at night I lie awake
I pray your love I will always keep
I reach out to touch your hand
and fall gently back to sleep.

THE CUCKOO AND THE NIGHTINGALE

Open all your windows and leave your doors ajar
listen to the melodic splendour that greets you from afar.

Through the woodland, down the lane, over hill and vale
sings the king of summer song the joyful Nightingale.

Rival to the pole position in both reputation and in song
the first two bars of summers symphony sing out as days grow long.

CUCKOO   CUCKOO   CUCKOO

But how can this have happened? it is all a feeble lie. The Cuckoo
deserves no such credit for it is the pirate of the sky.

Hawk like in its appearance the deception starts to falter
add child neglect and murder to the charge of original usurper.

Yet such deception is not confined to nature as you indeed will find,
for in our search for happiness we will meet many of a different kind.

But love and happiness awaits those who can say, without fail
they have learned to spot the difference between the Cuckoo
and the Nightingale.

A DOORWAY FOR A HOME

A doorway for a home
A box in which to bed
A street on which to beg upon
In the hope I'll soon be fed.

An empty cap that lies in hope
Of a momentary jingle
A saddened face a lonely heart
Warmed only by a candle.

Behind a shop a swollen bin
A search for any scraps
Is this not evolution in reverse?
Homo Sapiens versus alley cats.

An unexpected passer- by has filled my empty coffer.
There's always one (thank god for them)
Others pass me by and call me a dosser.

A doorway for a home
A box in which to bed
A street on which to beg upon
In the hope I'll soon be fed

An empty cap that lies in hope
Of a momentary jingle.
A saddened face a lonely heart
warmed only by a candle.

WHADDON WAY

The streets were empty back then
there was not a car in sight.
The men folk drove off to work every morning
and returned with their cars at night.

Few woman worked full time back then
and even fewer were able to drive,
So with the Town Centre two miles away,
many relied on the mobile shops to keep
them alive.

There was a butchers van and a bakers van too,
but there was one van in particular that everyone
waited eagerly to view .
Dan and his big green grocers van.
This cheerful portly chap always had a queue,
a meeting place for mothers and a welcome- break
from the many chores they had to do

This was the Whaddon Way of the early 1960's
Drabbles golden highway.
The main artery of the West Bletchley Estates
as it remains to this very day.

The sound of the buses that rattled along and
ferried the people to town.
The 394, the 395, the 396 and 397.
All long gone and now confined to transport heaven.

There is one childhood memory that will always linger on.
An annual event, on a cold, damp and foggy November day.
When Father Christmas, in his coach and horse's, rode slowly
down Whaddon Way.

A TEMPORARY CITY

Bletchley for Milton Keynes.
That is what it once said on the platform of our station.
Although I must admit there were those who were happy
with this status elevation.
but not for long, for they soon began to realize that
we were being treated like idol fools.
First our shops began to disappear, then so too did our schools.

A temporary city that is all we were, with no purpose and no worth.
To add insult to our injury, most of us were present at the City Centres
birth.

We were then invited to its Christening and went along, like we oughta,
only to find our own town centre was to be thrown out with the holy
bath water.

The Oxford Street of the charity world that is all we are now
a second hand city, in a second class town.

What would Winston Churchill have said? As he walked down to the
George, for a pint of the local bevvy.
If I could have told him that forty years from now his golden goose
would suffer urban rape and pillage.
Then have its identity hijacked by a tiny unknown village.

Milton Keynes! Whose idea was that? Surely Bletchley City
should have had a few takers.
A just reward for the town that helped save the world
as the home of the Code breakers.

If I were a little younger with an inclination towards anarchy
I would climb onto the platform at the city station and write
Milton Keynes for BLETCHLEY CITY.

If a friend in need
asked of me one deed
to define most accurately
a word he had heard
namely beautiful.
I would take him no further
than thee.

The Classroom

As I look around me my heart is filled with envy.
Happy faces waiting patiently to embark on life's
great journey.

That sense of evolving aspirations and untapped
ambition that represents, all that I once said and
all that I once did.

But oh what treasures I would trade, if just once
more, I could be a kid.

Should I Believe

Should I believe in a love that is true?
For there can be no guarantee
Only the hope that we'll stay the course
Right on to eternity.

Should I believe in a dream that is real?
At the risk of complacency
Taking for granted the feelings within
Though we know nothing of what is to be.

Should I believe that we are never to part
With no tears to cry, and no broken heart?
Or could it be, that one far off day
Another will come to steal you away.

I thank god for the pain I feel in my heart,
For it is loves way of telling us
How much it would hurt, if ever we did part.

What is the point

What is the point? What is its function?
This iconic landmark that once served
as the cities entertainment junction.

It now looks shabby, tired and weary
and when all is said and done.
It now stands in danger of becoming
the countries youngest slum.
Does anybody care? Or are we all smitten
with the knowledge that we now possess
the greenest cows in Britain.

In a roundabout way it is indicative of our
modern society that we should desert our past
before it has even reached maturity.

Don't look the other way, there can be no escape,
but of course there is an Xscape, which only begs
The question. What is the point?

Getting old

I'm getting old; it's there for all to see.
My reflection in the mirror bears no
resemblance to the face I used to see.

The pretty heads that I once turned have
long since turned away. As my withered
features fold an droop and my hair goes thin
and grey.

The hopes and dreams that once drove me on
were quickly overtaken
by daily life and the constant
need to make a living.

Are we born to live? Or are we born to die?
Are we heading for a destination that is preset?
Or are we heading swiftly for life's nearest exit.

It is all too easy to shrink from view or hide away
Just because we are getting older.
so come on you oldies, it is time to make a stand
And be a little bolder

ECLIPSE

The day the darkness fell

I stood upon the hill and looked out into the valley.
My erratic heart forewarned and feared for this the stricken alley.

I stood motionless, both excited and afraid, as in the distance I did see
a solid wall of darkness racing through the valley, as if intent on me.

Shrieks of nature filled the air in the blackened world that spelt
confusion.

While frenzied flights to who knows where? Bore evidence to nature's
greatest intrusion.

Silence fell upon the world as it waited in the wings, prepared for
retribution.

While I took comfort in human knowledge and waited for the inevitable
Solution.

DAYLIGHT

The love Rat

Honesty is not one of my strong points, but do you really want to know?
You may think I am carefree and exciting, but that to isn't so.
You have already formed the opinion that I am not your average guy.
Go ahead; feel free, for it is on your own self deception
that my ultimate success must rely.

You were no doubt informed, when you first came here, that I am a liar
on the lookout for my next bit of skirt.
So in a few weeks, when I tell you it's all over, it would not be deemed
wise to make a big show of your hurt.

Life can be dull and repetitive. It is all too easy to live for the dream.
So why should I be made to feel guilty? if your reputation should be
Tainted and demeaned.

Who cares if I hear a good story then pass it off as one of my own.
Or pretend I have suffered a great tragedy to stir the emotions of a
potential "loved one." Or if I should gaze into your eyes and promise
you the world, with a look of unquestionable sincerity. While knowing,
only too well, that I said something similar to another, only yesterday.

But then, in my life I have lost so much, while in pursuit of those I both
lied to and despised. A fantasy that proved to be fatal to the one true
love, I should have guarded with my life.

It all seems so pointless, I can't------wow! A gorgeous blond has just
passed me by, with a body to die for, a real feast for the eye.
Sorry, there's no time to lose. I really must fly.

Wandering eyes

If my eyes should ever wander
My head would turn them back
My heart would know the reason why
You keep my life on track.

I Used to know him rather well

I used to know him rather well.
We called him jokey Joe.
A laugh a minute type of guy,
that everyone would want know.

He worked on the machine next to mine,
and we always had a lark.
Teasing the ladies about the things
we got up to after dark.

We'd make out we were some kind of studs,
forever at the ready.
and delight at their response,
as our flirting made them feel rather heady.

But all that's changed, for he is now
just plain Mr. Dipple.
The nameplate sits firmly on his office door
and no-one dares to quibble.

He hardly manages a smile now,
as he passes by my way.
Discussing with his superior,
the business of the day.

Whenever I am asked who he is
I just look up and tell.
That once a long, long, time ago,
I used to know him rather well.

A Monument to my own perfection

I am neither black or white,
pink or yellow, red or green
or even a shade that is a tad in-between.

I exist only as a voice
that speaks from within
a vehicle for my opinions
oblivious to my skin.

To me I stand alone as a monument
to my own perfection.
Aware, that all around are others
who strive to make the same connection.

But he is black yes, him standing by the door
and with him is that yellow girl
next to that brown boy, and look there's
many more.

Why do they wear those funny clothes
and him that stupid hat?
And the food that they are eating
I've heard is strangled cat.

What's that, oh no my dear, I'm not prejudiced.
In fact, I am as tolerant as any other.
The comments I have made have nothing to do
race or colour. Have they ?

The Jolly Santa

There is a jolly Santa at a place I like to go.
I know it isn't really him of course
but he does remind me of him so.
With long white hair and flowing beard
he's altogether a very cuddly man.
He is my grandad of course and
Mrs Christmas is my Gran.

He doesn't treat me like my dad
who sometimes gets impatient and calls me dim.
once Grandad told me a secret (whispered)
he said when my dad was young he was Santa clause to him.
oh how much I'd like to see him standing in my room.
His smiling face and presence would be enough to lift me
from even the deepest gloom.

An apology for an anthology

They said it isn't poetry
They said it isn't verse.
A kind of working class mumbo jumbo
with no relevance and no worth.
They said you preyed on people's dreams
a kind of literary predator
and beside you in your evil scheme
your forever nodding editor.

The highbrow class, have had their noses
put well and truly out of joint.
Poetry is not theirs by right
and now they've finally got the point.
Soon the high street stores will fill their shelves
with copies of your anthologies.
What price false accusation, what justice in apology.

The highbrow class may once have caused our heads to bow
No more for that was poetry then
and this is poetry now.

The page of life

Of all the things we vowed to share
it seems our age is neither here nor there.
For I am twenty two and you are twenty one
a six month difference so evident since our time began.

But once a year on this fair day
love does find its own sweet way
to show to you what is good and true.
For today my love you are also twenty two.

Soon the page of life will turn
and for this day again I'll yearn,
but with you near the pain I will bear
until again our age we share.

Days gone by

Often my thoughts have turned to days gone by.
When a man, for no more than his faith, was prepared
to die.

And all for an ideal for which there can be no proof
just his honour and pride to keep him aloof.
To renounce his beliefs would mean to live a lie
a refusal to do so would mean he surely must die.
tight lipped he would sit not a word to be heard
What a waste, how stupid, how absurd.

But what if the man in this story were I
and my command, to renounce my love for you
or I to must surely die.

Suddenly my mind is filled with a fury
no god, man or king would I accept as a jury.
I begin to realize from deep inside
for the sake of a love maybe I to could have died.

King Richard The Nerd

If William Shakespeare is to be believed
King Richard the Third should have been titled
King Richard the Nerd.

His portrayal of a humpty backed, frail, beady eyed monster.
Who could murder his nephews, with no fear of his feeling guilty,
has long since been recognized for what it is, a mere Tudor fantasy

Consider, if you will, the following possibility.
A pact between a reluctant boy king and his uncle
that would ensure the boys safety and stability.

All that would be necessary to bring this plan to life
was a search to locate a couple of royal look-alikes.
Having collected the poor souls from Stony Stratford
Richard raced them to the Tower.
Where at some later date, he dispatched with them at
(you've guessed it) some unearthly hour.

What happened to the royal brothers? No one knows.
But I heard tell of a midnight cruise in Central Milton Keynes
known locally as the Battle of Cosworth. Where one young racer
whose engine had failed climbed from his stricken car and cried,
"A PORSHE A PORSHE MY KINGDOM FOR A PORSHE."

Is this fact or fiction? This royal story, that I tell you all?
Or is just in fact, another load of cock and bull.

REALITY

I had a dream. The dream came true,
but it turned into a nightmare.
And so to compensate I replaced my dream
with a fantasy. So far from view I could never
reach there.

Buried in an unreal world of self imposed isolation.
I rumbled on, still believing in my dream, my imaginative folly serving
as my only consolation.
Unaware the world looked on envious of my situation,
believing that I portrayed a rock stood upon the firmest foundation.

Then to my surprise my fantasy became a minor possibility.
Though in truth, I was in no way prepared for this eventuality.
For the fantasy I had invented was merely a device
to help me cushion the disappointment in my troubled life.

My dream then began to take on a better shape.
as if to confound my new dilemma
fantasy or reality what should I choose whichever is my better.

Seven days

God could not have
created the universe
in seven days.

It would have required
at least a week
to deliver all the love
I feel for you.

A place so far away

A place so far away
a time so long ago.
A fading memory
soon to be forgotten
with so little left that we know.

We bought our clothes from Roadnights
and put our fashions out on show.
then placed our heads in the record booths
over the road, on the corner, at Carlow's
A few short steps on to the Co-op
where we drank at the trendy milk bar
then down the high street to watch the latest films
at our very own cinema.

Then on to Central Gardens to swim in the outdoor pool
and afterwards to good old Makarios for a game on the pin ball.
We did not think about tomorrow, we lived only for the day.
and now I am in my sixties, I ask myself, was there really
any other way?

Beautiful You

Beautiful you so beautifully new
a fountain of softness and warmth.
A delicate cloud a soft silken shroud
to lie down on, or to adorn.

A magical smile to tempt and beguile
all that would stray into your territory.
And with Mother nature's best you embark
on your quest, to find your own true love
story.

Beautiful you so beautifully new
you will soon find your own place in time.
I'll have no fear, for I will stay here and keep
beautiful you to myself.

Of faults galore
I might complain
but without you near
I would live my life
in vain.

Valentine

A Valentine, so it is said,
should ideally be
an admirer incognito
shrouded in mystery.

An acquaintance or a colleague
or perhaps a friend of some note,
privately wishing his heart to you
he could devote.

A mere glimpse is enough to light
the flame of desire.
triggering the fantasy to which he would
hope to aspire.

You may well have spoken,
on this very day, and laughed loud
and hearty in an innocent way.

Unknown passions quickly aroused.
Passions, were they discovered,
might well be cruelly doused.
or perhaps not? Good luck.

Wacky Reputation

It isn't really that different
despite its wacky reputation.
There is a good array of high
street stores and an impressive
railway station.

From the air, on a good clear day,
CMK looks like it has been plucked
Straight from the Nevada desert in the
good old USA.

With its boulevard this and boulevard that
you could become confused, and wonder
where you are.
And with the noughts and crosses
road system it's a nightmare, even
with a car.

With a crystal palace for a shopping mall,
a top hat for a theatre and a giant slug
for a cinema. I suppose it is quite unique.
So if you're in the area, at any time, why not
come along and take a peek.

THE DAY THE QUEEN POPPED IN FOR TEA

I am not sure which house it was
so I have just come down to see
if I can find the house where the
Queen once popped in for tea.

On the green opposite Castles School
there was erected a large marquee
where the Queen met the oldest resident
and many a local dignitary.

There must have been some local envy
or even raging jealousy
as nearby neighbours commented;
why them, why not me?

I wouldn't know who lives there now
or if they know of its royal history
that once a long long time ago
the Queen popped in for tea.

THOUGHTS OF CRIME WRITER

By day my life is much like anybody else's.
However, at night, I stalk the streets in search of my
next victim. Such is the life of an aspiring crime
writer.

But is there something more sinister to all this
imaginary blood and guts? Perhaps it is a symptom
of an unhealthy interest, or worse still, a kind of
release valve for deeply held desires, surely not?

In fiction, the murderer is often portrayed as having
just cause for his actions. At the same time, the
victim seems to get what he deserves, a strange
morality indeed. Of course, he could well be a she.
After all, in the interest of equality and indeed equal
opportunities, the top job in a crime novel should be
open to all.

It is only left for me to ask myself this one question.
Is it foul play or mere folly? Are we providing
innocent entertainment for our readers.
Or are we just an evil bunch of closet murderers?

The Devil's Roundabout

It stood in the middle of a kiddies playground.
Which in hindsight, seemed a strange location
to place a so-called children's ride that had
earned itself an awesome reputation.

It stood in Leon Recreation Ground
the left hand corner is where it sat
You'd be cautious as you approached it
for this was the evil witches hat.

Spinning round and round, up and down,
in and out, with an undulating motion.
Throwing your senses into disarray
while in the grip of the witches potion.

Alton Towers, Blackpool and Thorpe park
all claim the country's most thrilling ride.
Well, let them slug it out and argue, tit for tat.
For how can they ever be sure; if they have
never had a ride on the witches hat.

BLETCHLEY PARK

Turn off the lights and show
Some respect for the dark.
Give all the help you can to
Those who work in the park.

Decode and decypher
As we constantly try for
The message that would
Bring an end to this war.

A combination of numbers
A sequence of letters
Or, if we are lucky, one
Unholy great flaw.

That would save thousands
of lives and bring home
Husbands to their wives
And lead our brave men
Straight to Hitler's front door.

Turn out the lights and show
Some respect for the dark
Let those who have been chosen
Get on with their work at the park.

TOWN OR CITY?

It's a Town.
No, it's a City.
It's a Town.
Actually, it's a Borough.

It's a City. It clearly say's so
On the boundary road signs.
The Borough and New City.

I understand it would require
Some kind of royal proclamation.
And I don't recall hearing such an
Important piece of information.

Whatever the situation,
It really is a pity.
The original intention
Was clearly stated.
It was to be a New City.

Church Green Road

If you were to don a blindfold
And were taken for a "little ride"
Then with your blindfold removed
You might very well decide.

You are in a village or a hamlet
Or miles out in the countryside.
But no, this rural scene of old
Is in the middle of a busy town
And it is known as Church Green Road.

Walk a few hundred yards in any direction
And you come across a vast estate.
Built to house the ever growing population
Whatever it may take.

An idyllic island, set within a Town
and County planners wildest dreams.
An oasis, or perhaps a mirage, in the
New City of Milton Keynes.

TATTENHOE LANE

BY

FLOYD COGGINS

A SHORT EXTRACT

CIRCA 1854

Maria stood at her bedroom window and looked out at the breathtaking view. Her heart filled with despair. Lazio was becoming ever more depressed by her inability to conceive, and she was beginning to feel his resolve failing. Few words had been exchanged in the past few days, and she knew something had to give.

She sighed a somber sigh, turned, and lay down upon the troubled marital bed. If only she could find a way to bring back the happiness she once shared with her husband. Her somber train of thought was soon interrupted by a gentle knock on her bedroom door. It was a sound that she had been dreading, for Lazio had made it clear that his patience was coming to an end and he had spent the last two hours in the library, pacing up and down trying to decide the best course of action he should take. She lifted herself from the bed and arranged herself into as presentable appearance as she could under the circumstances. "Come "she called out to Lazio. He entered the room hesitantly and took up a conciliatory, yet commanding, stance. Maria stood expressionless fearing the worst, she did not expect to be Mrs. Verdi for much longer, for, despite her husband's Catholic status, she knew her inability to conceive, matched with his powerful family connections, could be combined to attempt to gain a special dispensation from the pope, leading directly to an annulment of their marriage.

Lazio looked toward the heavens, as if in despair, and then began to say his piece: "I have come to the only decision in this sorry matter that my conscious will allow me. I cannot betray your fathers trust without at least one more try. Therefore I will stay for twelve more months in the hope that conception will take place. If indeed it does not, I will have no choice but to take my leave of you and apply for an annulment." Maria showed no sign of emotion, but, inside, her heart was filled with joy and relief as she replied. "I could have asked for no more in these circumstances than your continued patience. I thank you whole- heartedly for that. You are indeed a man of honour and I will not fail you again. Should I not conceive, I will release you from all obligations toward me, albeit with much regret."

Lazio gently nodded his head in gratitude and left the room. Maria clasped her hands in relief, and pressing them against her lips, she paced up and down desperately searching for a way out of her situation. Over the years, she had toyed with many schemes and followed to the letter many old wives tales in an attempt to give the man she loved the children he so desperately wanted, all had failed miserably. All, that is except the one scheme she hardly dared to consider, the one that lurked deep in her subconscious and only showed itself in her dreams. The one that involved kidnap and murder, If she left it to nature the chances are she would be left with no child and no husband, after all if five years were not enough for her to conceive, another twelve months wasn`t likely to be either.

This was the first time that she had ever dared to consider the unthinkable option, which now seemed to be the only possible solution left open to her. She began to explore the ways and means that she would have to follow to secure a successful conclusion. Guided only by the memories of her recurring dream, her plan began to take shape.

VERNEY JUNCTION

BY

FLOYD COGGINS

A SHORT EXTRACT

As much as Staye loved hearing Tom's tales of old, he could not see how he could justify staying in Verney Junction any longer, while a mad murderer was running around on his patch. "I would love to stay and listen to your delightful stories, but I think the good Sergeant should return us to Winslow, where we can evaluate what we have heard. Thank you for your help." Sally showed them to the door and then wished them well with their investigation. Then the three men left and made their way toward the car. As they were about to depart, Staye saw Sally Lane running towards them holding a book. Staye wound down the window, as Sally said, "This book might be of help it was written by Perkins son. It's an account of his father's time at Verney and is full of old photos and fascinating facts." Staye took the book and thanked Sally. They all drove off in the direction of Winslow. As they drove off,

Staye began to flick through the pages of the book Sally had just given them.

While he was flicking through the pages, Staye became aware that something he had seen in the book was troubling him, though he did not know what it was, or where in the book he had seen whatever it was. Repeatedly, he was drawn to page ten where a picture of a woman, hanging out her washing in the garden, filled the whole page. Underneath the photo was a written caption that explained the scene clearly, and said, "Mother in the garden of the original Station house hanging out the weekly washing, while Father, (who is not visible) is busy working in the cellar that he used as a darkroom for his great passion photography. Only the half- open wooden cellar door holds the clue to his whereabouts and activity." Suddenly, it hit him like a bolt of lightning, as he cried out, "Stop the car now, we are going back to Verney." Plumrose slammed on the brakes and the car skidded to a halt. "What the hell is going on?" Asked Det Shaw. Staye handed him the book and pointed to the photo. Shaw looked confused. "It`s just a photo of a woman hanging out her clothes." Staye pointed at two trees that grew next to each other and had branches that met above the half-open cellar door. "That one is an apple tree and the one next to it is a pear tree. You will find it all there under an apple and pear, remember?" Shaw looked again at the picture in the book and said, "You're right, we had better go back and find the cellar and see what is inside.

Sgt Plumrose turned the car around and headed once again for Verney Junction. Within minutes they were back in Verney Junction and, having left the car outside the station house, they walked along the mud track that led to the now almost non-existent Station. As they passed the house Sally Lane caught a glimpse of them, and curious to see why they had returned she hurried out of the house to catch them. The three men climbed onto the grass and moss covered platform that once housed, a waiting room, buffet, toilets and even an ornamental garden. Which in its hey-day, had earned the title of Best-kept Station. By now, Sally had caught up with them and filled with curiosity, she asked, "Why are you back?" Staye peered up the track and replied, "Where did you say this old Station house stood?" Sally pointed up the track and replied, "It's where you can see the track separate from the main line. That is where the sidings were, but there is no sign of the old house, the track is laid over it. Dad reckons the ten yards or so of space between the two lines is where the old garden was."

Staye turned to Sgt Plumrose and said, "Sergeant, I want you to go back to Winslow and arrange for a large contingent of officers, from the surrounding area, to come out here as soon as possible to help us locate the old cellar." Then turning to Shaw, he said, "Dave I want you to go back to the Station house with Sally to ring the chief. Ask him to get down here as soon as possible." Shaw looked at Staye in a hesitant way and replied, "Are you sure, sir, I mean we haven't found anything yet." Staye again looked up the track and replied, "If I am wrong, I will look a right prat, but if I am right the chief will be more than thankful that I called him down here."

It was fast approaching midday and the sun was beating down on the once busy track causing it to appear bent and distorted in the distant haze. Staye contemplated the future events that could yet unfold. Ninety minutes had passed since Plumrose had returned to Winslow, and Staye was beginning to wonder where he was, when suddenly, in the distance, in a scene reminiscent of an old western the cavalry appeared with sirens screaming as they raced to the scene. Sgt Plumrose had never known the likes of it and he was enjoying every moment. At last, he felt like a real police officer. Within minutes of arriving Staye and Shaw had organised the men into two groups, both clearing the dense undergrowth that had covered the relevant area, over the many years that had passed. Their one mission was to find any evidence of an old cellar door.

Any hopes of a speedy discovery were soon laid to rest as forty-five minutes went by with nothing found. As if to confound the situation, the arrival of a furious Chief Insp Lawson only served to add to the already unbearable tension. Staye could see that the approaching chief was not a happy man. As he reached them, he let rip at Staye, "What the bloody hell is the idea of dragging me down to this God-forsaken hell-hole of a place?" He then paused for a second, his face red with anger, before continuing, "My God Staye this had better be good." he concluded. Staye crossed his fingers and replied, "Sir, I believe that in an old cellar somewhere over there. We will find the body of one Susan Jones, who went missing in 1967."

Had Staye said the wrong thing or what? The chief bellowed at the top of his voice, "More bodies, I sent you down here to find the murderer, not more bodies. If I had wanted more bodies I would have gone to a bloody mortuary," he added furiously. Just then, and to Stayes relief, the chief's rage was interrupted by one of the digging constables, who shouted, "I've found a hatch or something, sir."Plumrose, Staye, Shaw and the chief all ran over to where the constable had been digging and peered down at the closed hatch door. "Shall I open it?" said the officer hesitantly. Staye nodded, the air filled with tension, as the officer took hold of the handle. To everyone's surprise, the hatch door opened easily. At first sight, it was hard to see clearly into the cellar, but as the sun emerged from the clouds the secret of the cellar was revealed. No one was prepared for the sight that befell them. Sergeant Plumrose gasped, the young constable fainted, and Sally Lane collapsed in a heap. Down in the cellar was a mountain of skeletons, suitcases, hats and shoes. Staye looked at the chief in an almost apologetic way and said, "We could shut it up and pretend we didn't find it, if you like, sir." Amazingly, enough the chief's anger subsided at the horrific sight before them, as he went into an overdrive of procedure. "Cordon off the whole area, no one comes in or out, without my say so. Send for forensics straight away, pathology too, and arrange a press conference for the morning. Oh, and Sgt Plumrose, we will need an incident room, a hall or something."

Staye stood almost motionless looking into the cellar. He had suspected something sinister, but not even in is wildest dreams had he expected this. Plumrose and his colleagues were still doing their best to comfort the, by now, conscious constable, while Staye had Sally Lane cradled in his arms, as he tried to revive her. As she began to come round her eyes opened and she stared up at Stayes face, "Tell me I dreamt it all," she said, hopefully. Staye could offer no such assurance, as he replied, "I wish I could tell you what you want to hear, but unfortunately I cannot." He helped Sally to her feet and asked Plumrose to escort her back to the house and then return. As Plumrose left, with Sally heading for the old Station house. Chief Inspector Lawson pushed shut the cellar hatch. "I think we'll give them an hour or so of peace before we start bringing them up," he said, respectfully.

Staye, Lawson, and Shaw stood quietly together looking down at the cellar door, their minds ablaze with questions and possibilities. Shaw began to scratch his head nervously and said, "Where the hell do we go from here?" Lawson looked hopefully toward Staye, now more than ever he hoped that Staye's intuition had something more to offer. "Charles Perkins," replied Staye. The chief looked confused. "Who the hell is Charles Perkins?" he said. Staye interrupted immediately, "He is the son of the Station Master who worked here before the station house was moved to its present location. Moreover, as far as I can see, he is the only man alive who would have known of the cellars existence. That is, of course, if he is still alive." Shaw looked a little confused, "We don't know where he is, sir." He said. Staye opened the book that Sally had given them and replied, "No but his publisher will and the address is printed here on the first page. Jacobs Publishing, Trent House, Bleeding heart yard Holborn, let's get going," he concluded. "Hold on a minute sir, we could ask Tom or Sally Lane, surely." Staye paused for a second and then explained, "We don't know who has done all this, everyone is a suspect at this stage and I can't risk anyone knowing our next move, in case one warns another." Shaw, realising that his boss was right nodded.

John Staye and Dave Shaw set off immediately to retrieve their car from outside The Verney Arms. Then, within minutes, they were on their way to Jacobs Publishing in the hope of finding Charles Perkin's home address. In the meantime, Sergeant Plumrose had returned from escorting Sally Lane to the station house and reported immediately to Chief Inspector Lawson. He was quite short of breath from the exertion of rushing around; it was certainly not your average working day in Winslow Town. "The Thames Valley Murder Squad are on their way from Reading sir. A Chief Inspector Day is bringing them up, and I have requisitioned the function room at The Verney Arms. The landlord is a friend of mine. It is self- contained and separated from the pub by a locked door. It will make an excellent incident room and we can move straight in." Chief Inspector Lawson smiled politely and replied, "Well done Sergeant, "if I could leave it to you to make the necessary arrangements for the installations and equipment that will be needed to carry out, what may be a long and protracted investigation.

GONE BUT NOT FORGOTTEN.

BAKERS FIELD

BUCKINGHAM ROAD

BLETCHLEY

MANY A SUMMER PICNIC.

SIMPSON ROAD

OPPOSITE WHADDON WAY

UNDER THE RAILWAY BRIDGE

MANY A BIKE RIDE TO THE CANAL.

WOLVERTON OPEN AIR POOL

THE BEST DAY OUT

IN THE AREA

ON A HOT SUMMER DAY

CO-OP DEPARTMENT STORE

BLETCHLEY

EVERYTHING UNDER ON ROOF

COLDHARBOUR PIT

GREAT FISHING

FREEZING COLD SWIMMING

BLETCHLEY AND DISTRICT SPORTS DAY

LEON RECREATION GROUND

BLETCHLEY.

THE SUMMER OF 1976

WOW!

WOLVERTON SCOUT HUT DISCO

GREAT NIGHT

WEDNESDAYS (I THINK)

FRIDAY NIGHT DISCO

BLETCHLEY YOUTH CENTRE

AN ABSOLUTE MUST

CALIFORNIA BALLROOM

ANY TIME

DUNSTABLE

THE BLETCHLEY GAZZETTE

EVERYTHING YOU NEEDED

TO KNOW

LOCALLY

Printed in Poland
by Amazon Fulfillment
Poland Sp. z o.o., Wrocław

49233684R00040